TINTIN'S TRAVEL DIARIES

Publisher's note:

Tintin, the intrepid reporter, first made his appearance January 10, 1929, in a serial newspaper strip with an adventure in the Soviet Union. From there, it was on to the Belgian Congo and then to America. Together with his dog, Snowy; an old seaman, Captain Haddock; an eccentric professor, Cuthbert Calculus; look-alike detectives, Thomson and Thompson; and others, Tintin roamed the world from one adventure to the next.

Tintin's dog, Snowy, a small white fox terrier, converses with Tintin, saves his life many times, and acts as his confidant, despite his weakness for whiskey and a tendency toward greediness. Captain Haddock, in some ways Snowy's counterpart, is a reformed lover of whiskey, with a tendency toward colorful language and a desire to be a gentleman-farmer. Cuthbert Calculus, a hard-of-hearing, sentimental, absent-minded professor, goes from small-time inventor to nuclear physicist. The detectives, Thomson and Thompson, stereotyped characters down to their old-fashioned bowler hats and outdated expressions, are always chasing Tintin. Their attempts at dressing in the costume of the place they are in make them stand out all the more.

The Adventures of Tintin appeared in newspapers and books all over the world. Georges Remi (1907–1983), better known as Hergé, based Tintin's adventures on his own interest in and knowledge of places around the world. The stories were often irreverent, frequently political and satirical, and always exciting and humorous.

Tintin's Travel Diaries is a new series, inspired by Hergé's characters and based on notebooks Tintin may have kept as he traveled. Each book in this series takes the reader to a different country, exploring its geography, and the customs, the culture, and the heritage of the people living there. Hergé's original cartooning is used, juxtaposed with photographs showing the country as it is today, to give a feeling of fun as well as education.

If Hergé's cartoons seem somewhat out of place in today's society, think of the time in which they were drawn. The cartoons reflect the thinking of the day, and set next to modern photographs, we learn something about ourselves and society, as well as about the countries Tintin explores. We can see how attitudes have changed over the course of half a century.

Hergé, himself, would change his stories and drawings periodically to reflect the changes in society and the comments his work would receive. For example, when it was originally written in 1930, *Tintin in the Congo*, on which *Tintin's Travel Diaries: Africa* is based, was slanted toward Belgium as the fatherland. When Hergé prepared a color version in 1946, he did away with this slant. Were Hergé alive today, he would probably change many other stereotypes that appear in his work.

From the Congo, Tintin went on to America. This was in 1931. Al Capone was notorious, and the idea of cowboys and Indians, prohibition, the wild west, as well as factories, all held a place of fascination. *Cigars of the Pharaoh* (1934) introduced Hergé's fans to the mysteries of Egypt and India. A trip to China came with *The Blue Lotus* in 1936, the first story Hergé thoroughly researched. After that, everything was researched, including revisions of previous stories. *The Land of Black Gold*, for example, an adventure in the Middle East, was written in 1939, and revised in 1949 and again in 1969.

Although *The Broken Ear* introduced readers to the Amazon region in 1935, the story was pure fantasy, complete with imaginary countries. In 1974 the adventure continued with *Tintin and the Picaros*, Hergé's last story. When *The Seven Crystal Balls*, which was serialized from 1943 to 1944, was continued in 1946, Hergé began to give the reader factual information about pre-Columbian civilization with marginal notes titled "Who were the Incas?" *Tintin in the Land of the Soviets* was Tintin's first adventure, in 1929, and the only one not to be redone in color.

Tintin's Travel Diaries are fun to read, fun to look at, and provide educational, enjoyable trips around the world. Perhaps, like Tintin, you, too, will be inspired to seek out new adventures!

The publisher particularly wishes to thank Mrs. Christine Ockrent and television channel Antenne 2 for their kind permission to use the title *Travel Diaries*.

RUSSIA

TINTIN'S TRAVEL DIARIES

A collection conceived and produced by Martine Noblet.

Les films du sable thank the following **Connaissance du monde** *photographers for their participation in this work:*

Jean-Michel Bertrand, Claude Jannel, Michel Drachoussoff, Yves Sommavilla, and the Mahuzier family

The authors thank Daniel De Bruycker and Christiane Erard for their collaboration.

First edition for the United States and Canada published
by Barron's Educational Series, Inc., 1995.

All inquiries should be addressed to:
Barron's Educational Series, Inc.
250 Wireless Boulevard
Hauppauge, New York 11788

Library of Congress Catalog Card No. 94-41241

International Standard Book No. 0-8120-6491-7 (hard cover)
International Standard Book No. 0-8120-9162-0 (paperback)

Library of Congress Cataloging-in-Publication Data

Deltenre, Chantal.
   Russia / text by Chantal Deltenre and Maximilian Dauber ;
translation by Maureen Walker.
      p.   cm. — (Tintin's travel diaries)
   Includes bibliographical references and index.
   ISBN 0-8120-6491-7 (cloth). — ISBN 0-8120-9162-2 (pbk.)
   1. Soviet Union—Description and travel—Juvenile literature.
[1. Soviet Union   2. Cartoons and comics.]   I. Dauber, Maximilien.
II. Walker, Maureen.   III. Title.   IV. Series
DK29.D45   1995
914.7—dc20   94-41241
                                                              CIP
                                                              AC

Printed in Hong Kong
5678   9927   987654321

RUSSIA

Text by Chantal Deltenre and Martine Noblet

Translation by Maureen Walker

BARRON'S

As a child, and a regular reader of your paper and your books, Hergé, I managed to get the first edition of *Tintin in the Land of the Soviets*, and gradually I acquired the entire adventure series.

The series enabled a friend of mine, who was an enthusiastic Latin scholar, to translate you into the language of Caesar. Tintin and Milou [Snowy] became "Tintinus Milusque," but adapting Captain Haddock's "expressions" was something of a problem. Indeed, the Bachi-Bouzouk soldiers, the Zouave tribe, and the iconoclast sect did not yet exist under the Roman Empire. The anarchist Ravachol, Rocambole, and the capuchin monkeys and phylloxera native to America were unknown, and the duck-billed platypus had not yet been identified.

My thanks to my pal Tintin for letting me illustrate this travel guide about Russia. Give Snowy a pat, and give Professor Calculus and fiery old Haddock a resounding greeting, from me.

CLAUDE JANNEL

When Hergé told the story of your adventures in Russia, Tintin, a lot of people said—and this went on for over 50 years—that you had exaggerated and perhaps even lied. Now everybody, or almost everybody, knows that what you said was true.

Tintin in the Land of the Soviets was your first big adventure and remains the least well known. The truth may not always be a good thing to tell…but what a lot of time wasted, tears shed, blood spilled, before the "opinion makers" admit their mistakes or their blindness…

Since your trip to the land of the Soviets, the world has changed a lot. Today, the Soviet Union no longer exists, the C.I.S. (Commonwealth of Independent States) doesn't yet really exist, and the Republic of Russia is trying to find itself and struggling to survive.

Tintin, it is a very great pleasure for me to be revisiting with you the Russia for which I inherited love and pride through my parents and grandparents.

MICHEL DRACHOUSSOFF

CONTENTS

The words in **boldface** refer to the glossary, beginning on page 70.

IS RUSSIA STILL THE BIGGEST COUNTRY IN THE WORLD?

The U.S.S.R.—for a long time the giant among the world's countries—divided into 15 independent countries in 1990. Today, the Republic of Russia is still the largest country in the world.

After the Bolshevik Revolution in 1917, the Empire of Russia became the U.S.S.R.—the Union of Soviet Socialist Republics. Stretching across two continents, the U.S.S.R. took up more than half of Europe and almost two-fifths of Asia. With its 13.75 million square miles (22 million sq. km), it covered a territory two and one-half times the size of the United States.

In 1990 the republics associated with Russia within the huge federation proclaimed their independence, and the U.S.S.R. split into 15 independent states. The Republic of Russia alone makes up more than three-fourths of the territory of the Union and is home to over 151 million people. With almost 11 million square miles (17 million sq. km), 30 times the size of Texas, it is the largest country in the world!

From west to east, from its borders with Norway, Finland, or Poland, to the Bering Strait separating it from Alaska, Russia covers more than 6,250 miles (10,000 km). From north to south, from the polar coasts of the Arctic Ocean to the deserts bordering the Caspian Sea, it covers 2,813 miles (4,500 km).

Left: The Ananouri Fortress in Georgia (Caucasus)
Right: St. Basil's Cathedral in Red Square, Moscow

WHICH IS THE COLDEST REGION IN RUSSIA?

In eastern Siberia, the thermometer falls on average to -59.8°F (-51°C) in January. It may even get down to -92.2°F (-69°C). That is real Siberian cold!

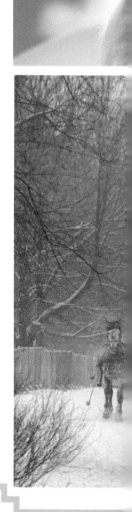

S iberia, which is near the North Pole, has a continental climate. The winter is harsh and the hot, dry summer lasts only two or three months. The earth does not have time to thaw out completely before the icy winds, called the *purga*, and the *burans* (blizzards) return. The ocean is not as cold in winter as the earth's crust, but it is too far away to moderate the temperature. Because of the frigid temperatures, it's not surprising that the Russians invented the *samovar*, a type of urn used to boil water for tea. Sheltered by the log walls of the **isba**, the entire household is warmed by the *petchka*, a stone or ceramic stove on which the bedding rests. When they leave the house, Russians put on fur hats called *chapkas* and bundle up in heavy felt coats or long cloaks.

In the past, people traveled in *troikas*, sleighs pulled by three horses. These were the only vehicles that could maneuver easily through the snowy countryside.

This rigorous climate, to some extent, is true of Russia as a whole. In Moscow, the temperature may fall to −40°F (−40°C), and sometimes the Sea of Azov, on the same latitude as northern Maine, is completely frozen.

Top: Yakut girl (Siberia)
Bottom left: A troika
Bottom right: A snow sculpture in
Novosibursk

HOW LONG IS THE VOLGA?

The Volga River rises in the hills of northern Russia and empties into the Caspian Sea after a 2,194 mile (3,531 km) course. It is the longest river in Europe.

B esides the Volga, the great rivers of the plains are the Don, the Dnieper, and the Ural. In summer, they are powerful channels of communication for barges that in the past were pulled along from the banks of the river by teams of haulers, whose suffering is evoked in the moving songs of the Volga boatmen.

Russia's icy climate makes these wide waterways unusable in winter until the spring thaw. Then the entire country becomes such an immense marshy wasteland that for many years Russians believed that the capricious mood of their rivers reflected that of gods, spirits, and fairies.

Even more feared are the rivers in Siberia: the Yenisey, the Ob, and the Lena. All three together are longer than the Volga, and flow northward, as far as the icy Arctic Ocean. In the spring, when the melting snow causes floods upstream, the water pours over the top of the ice, hampering their downstream course. Disastrous floods result because the frozen soil can absorb only a small amount of water.

The Lena River in Siberia

WHY IS THE BEREZINA FAMOUS?

The disastrous crossing of this little tributary of the Dnieper, in Byelorussia, was the final blow in the destruction of Napoleon's "Great Army," already defeated by the cruel winter, in the frozen expanse of the Russian plains.

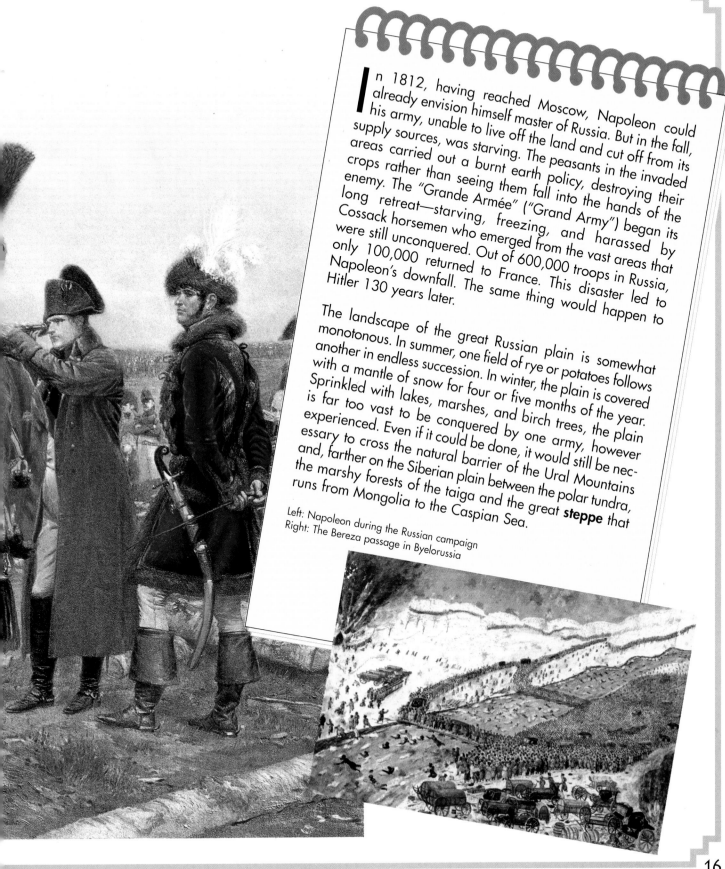

In 1812, having reached Moscow, Napoleon could already envision himself master of Russia. But in the fall, his army, unable to live off the land and cut off from its supply sources, was starving. The peasants in the invaded areas carried out a burnt earth policy, destroying their crops rather than seeing them fall into the hands of the enemy. The "Grande Armée" ("Grand Army") began its long retreat—starving, freezing, and harassed by Cossack horsemen who emerged from the vast areas that were still unconquered. Out of 600,000 troops in Russia, only 100,000 returned to France. This disaster led to Napoleon's downfall. The same thing would happen to Hitler 130 years later.

The landscape of the great Russian plain is somewhat monotonous. In summer, one field of rye or potatoes follows another in endless succession. In winter, the plain is covered with a mantle of snow for four or five months of the year. Sprinkled with lakes, marshes, and birch trees, the plain is far too vast to be conquered by one army, however experienced. Even if it could be done, it would still be necessary to cross the natural barrier of the Ural Mountains and, farther on the Siberian plain between the polar tundra, the marshy forests of the taiga and the great **steppe** that runs from Mongolia to the Caspian Sea.

Left: Napoleon during the Russian campaign
Right: The Bereza passage in Byelorussia

WHERE IS THE TUNDRA?

The tundra spreads over the extreme north of Russia. It is a treeless region, cold and windswept. Hardly anything is found there but moss, lichen, and, in summer, moors with ferns and tall grasses.

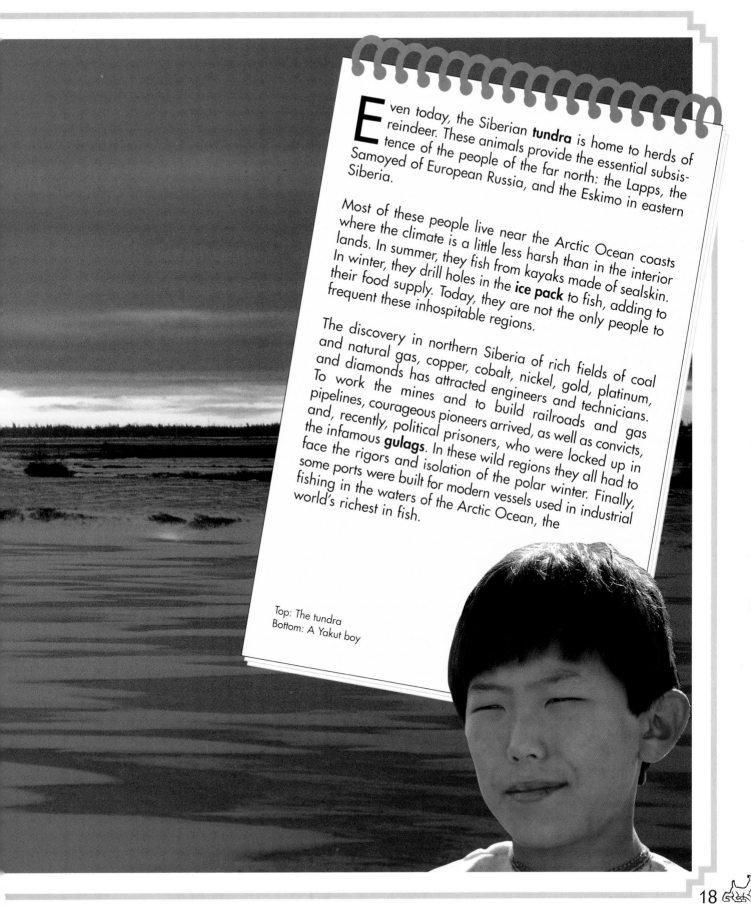

Even today, the Siberian **tundra** is home to herds of reindeer. These animals provide the essential subsistence of the people of the far north: the Lapps, the Samoyed of European Russia, and the Eskimo in eastern Siberia.

Most of these people live near the Arctic Ocean coasts where the climate is a little less harsh than in the interior lands. In summer, they fish from kayaks made of sealskin. In winter, they drill holes in the **ice pack** to fish, adding to their food supply. Today, they are not the only people to frequent these inhospitable regions.

The discovery in northern Siberia of rich fields of coal and natural gas, copper, cobalt, nickel, gold, platinum, and diamonds has attracted engineers and technicians. To work the mines and to build railroads and gas pipelines, courageous pioneers arrived, as well as convicts, and, recently, political prisoners, who were locked up in the infamous **gulags**. In these wild regions they all had to face the rigors and isolation of the polar winter. Finally, some ports were built for modern vessels used in industrial fishing in the waters of the Arctic Ocean, the world's richest in fish.

Top: The tundra
Bottom: A Yakut boy

18

WHAT ANIMALS LIVE IN THE TAIGA?

Between the tundra to the north and the grassy steppe to the south, there stretches a huge coniferous forest called the taiga. It covers two-thirds of the territory in both the European and Asiatic part of the country, and shelters many animals.

oodcutters and trappers, the people who in-habit the **taiga** have long made their living in the fur trade. They have always hunted fox and the precious sable, a marten that exists only in Russia. In ancient times, daring traders came from Greece, Persia, and even China to buy from them. But the forest is also home to many other wild animals: eland, deer, bear, and, much farther to the east, the powerful Siberian tiger.

These inhospitable forests, sometimes marshy and full of mosquitos, are considered the birthplace of the Russian people. Colonizing the grassy areas in the forest, small communities of peasants patiently cleared and enlarged their land to cultivate potatoes and vegetables, to raise some cattle, and to put in beehives.

Despite considerable development of the Russian country-side, the forest still covers vast expanses where wood remains the basic material used both to build isbas and to heat them in winter.

Top: A reindeer
Bottom: Russian brown bears

WHO ARE THE HORSEMEN OF THE STEPPE?

The great steppe of Asia extends from Manchuria to Europe. It has remained the home of nomads who raise horses, from the Huns and the Mongols so feared in the past to the Kazakhs, Turkmen, and Kirghiz of today.

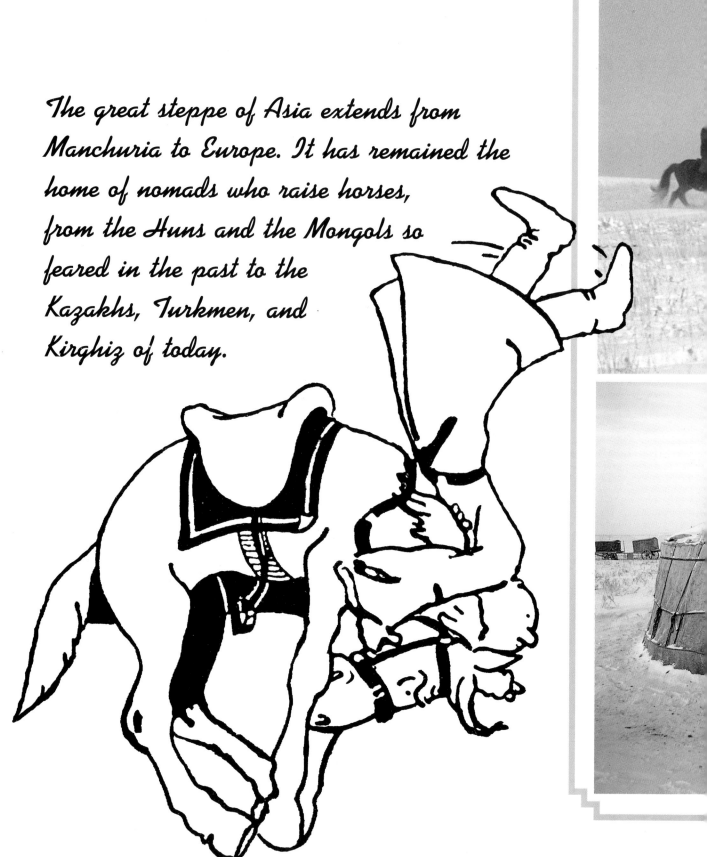

Seen from the air, the steppe (plain) looks like a sea of grass extending from east to west for 5,000 miles (8,000 km). Unusual animals can be found there, such as the saiga antelope with its rounded forehead, several species of wild donkeys, and the Przewaski horse, ancestor of the small horses ridden by the peoples of the steppe.

The life of the nomads, forever in search of pastures, and their love of horses make them excellent horsemen and feared warriors, long-suffering and disciplined. More than once in history, one leader was able to bring the scattered tribes together in a "horde" and set off to conquer neighboring countries: **Attila**'s Huns or **Gengis Khan**'s Mongols invaded China, India, Persia, and Russia, and we can't forget the **Scythians**, ancestors of the Bulgarians and Hungarians, the Kalmuks, and even the Manchus.

Today, the Kazakhs, Turkmen, Kirghiz, Tajiks, and Mongols are peaceful people who have regained their independence. Despite the pressure from Communist authorities to change their lifestyle, many have preserved their ancient traditions. They live in yurts, tents made of felt, and exist on the milk of their mares, from which they make yogurt. They drink *kumiss*, a sort of beer, and meet every year at the big markets to sell their animals.

Top: A herd of horses on the Mongolian steppes
Bottom: A Mongol in front of his yurt.

WHO WERE THE ANCESTORS OF THE RUSSIANS?

The Russians belong to the family of Slavic-speaking people who settled over 3,000 years ago throughout Eastern Europe. The name "Russian" is said to be a heritage from the Vikings, the first founders of Russia.

The Slavs are one of the branches of the Indo-European family, like the Aryans of India and Iran, or the Greeks, Latins, Germans, Celts, and Scandinavians.

While their cousins emigrated westward and southward, the Slavs stayed in their region of origin, in spite of new invasions from Asia that divided them into a number of groups. In the south were the Serbs and the Croats; farther west were the Poles, the Czechs, and the Slovaks. In the east were the Russians, also divided into three nations: those known today as Ukrainians, the "white" Russians of Byelorussia, (so-called because of the color of their traditional caps), and the forest-dwelling Russians, who are the actual Russians.

It was Vikings from Sweden, the Varangian Russes, who, plying the rivers aboard their trading vessels as far as the Black Sea, federated the diverse tribes of Russians into a powerful state capable of standing up to the nomads from central Asia. Thus the Varangian chieftain **Rurik**, who arrived in 862, became their first king, leaving, it is believed, the name of *Rus* (Varangian term for ruddy or fair men) to his kingdom and his people.

Top: A Russian boy wearing his *chapka*, traditional hat   Bottom: Russian people through the ages

WHICH ALPHABET IS USED IN RUSSIA?

The Cyrillic alphabet is not a Russian invention. It was created by the Greek monk, St. Cyril, and his brother, Methodius, to enable the Slavs who converted to Christianity to read the Bible.

Before the 800s, the Slavs spoke a number of different dialects and did not write. When St. Cyril and his brother Methodius wanted to teach the gospel to their Slavic disciples, they had to codify, unify, and provide writing for a new language—Slavonic.

Gradually changing, the Slavonic devised by the monks between 888 and 898 became the modern Russian language, still written with the alphabet created by St. Cyril. It resembles the Greek alphabet, but with the addition of several new letters that correspond to sounds belonging specifically to the Slavic languages, like the "shch" in the word **borshch** (or **borscht**).

At the end of the Middle Ages, Russian culture, cut off from the classical heritage of the West, went into a long period of stagnation. With a few exceptions, science and the modern ideas spreading over the West did not get through to Russia until 300 years later. The Tatars resisted Western influence during their reign, which lasted two centuries.

The Byzantine Empire made its way into the Eastern Slavic region in 988, influencing its religion and culture. In addition, with the establishment of the Slavic language and alphabet, scholars (generally members of the religious community) did not feel the need to learn Greek or Latin.

Left: A road sign in Armenia (Caucasus)

Right: A poster showing Cyrillic writing.

Top: Political slogans, no longer in existence, on buildings in St. Petersburg

WHAT IS AN ICON?

In the Eastern Orthodox tradition of Greece and Russia, an icon is a picture of Christ, of the Virgin Mary, or of a saint. Painted on wood and embellished with gold, it adorns churches and private houses.

The **Eastern Orthodox** church service includes much pomp, and the churches are absolute gems, full of icons, frescoes, and valuable treasures. The best known is St. Basil's, on Red Square in Moscow, with its many-colored, onion-domed towers.

The faith of the Eastern Orthodox Christians is very strong, and many communities of hermits, who may be either monks or laymen, impose upon themselves a life of very harsh penitence because of their love for God. Belief in the miraculous power of icons and saints remains deeply anchored in the faith of the people.

Because it aspires to being a **rationalist** philosophy, **communism** rejects belief in God; therefore, at the time of the Revolution in 1917, all religions were systematically persecuted in the U.S.S.R. Eastern Orthodox Christians, Jews, Roman Catholics, Muslims in Central Asia, Mongolian Buddhists, and Siberian Animists all had to pray and celebrate their rites in secret, deprived of most of their places of worship and of their priests. In spite of the Communist opposition, however, over 50 million people still belonged to the Eastern Orthodox Church by the 1980s. Today, all of the religions are emerging again.

Left: The Cathedral of the Assumption in Zagorsk
Above: An icon of the Virgin Mary

WHAT IS THE CAPITAL OF RUSSIA?

Though Moscow is not the geographical center of Russia, it is its capital. All the railroads, airlines, roads, and travelers meet or begin in this great city.

MOSCOW!

A meeting point of East and West, Moscow is a megalopolis of 9 million inhabitants, where all races rub shoulders and all languages are spoken. Though Leningrad, which has again become St. Petersburg, has retained its splendors from the past, Moscow has changed a great deal over the past 50 years. The wooden houses that gave the old city its charm have disappeared as well as many historic areas. Here, as in many modern cities, bulldozers have destroyed whole sections of history.

In Moscow there is more in the way of entertainment and important places to visit than anywhere else in the country. Red Square, famous the world over, has seen the great moments of Moscow and of all of Russia. It is from this square that people can go to visit the Kremlin, the Church of St. Basil the Blessed with its many-colored cupolas, or the Gum department store with its 1.56 mile (2.5 km) shopping mall. Visited every day by more than 350,000 people, it is the busiest store in all of Russia. Despite its many attractions, however, Moscow today is the heart of a republic in the midst of chaos. Capitalism gone wild, galloping inflation, and real estate speculation make Moscow a city where it is becoming harder and harder to find a place to live and even to get enough to eat.

Left: The Arbat, pedestrian walkway
Right: The huge department store "Gum"

WHAT DOES THE WORD "KREMLIN" MEAN?

During the troubled times of the Middle Ages, the fortress, or "kremlin," was the basis of all power. Since the czars, the Kremlin of the princes of Moscow has become the political center of Russia, surpassing those of Novgorod and Kiev.

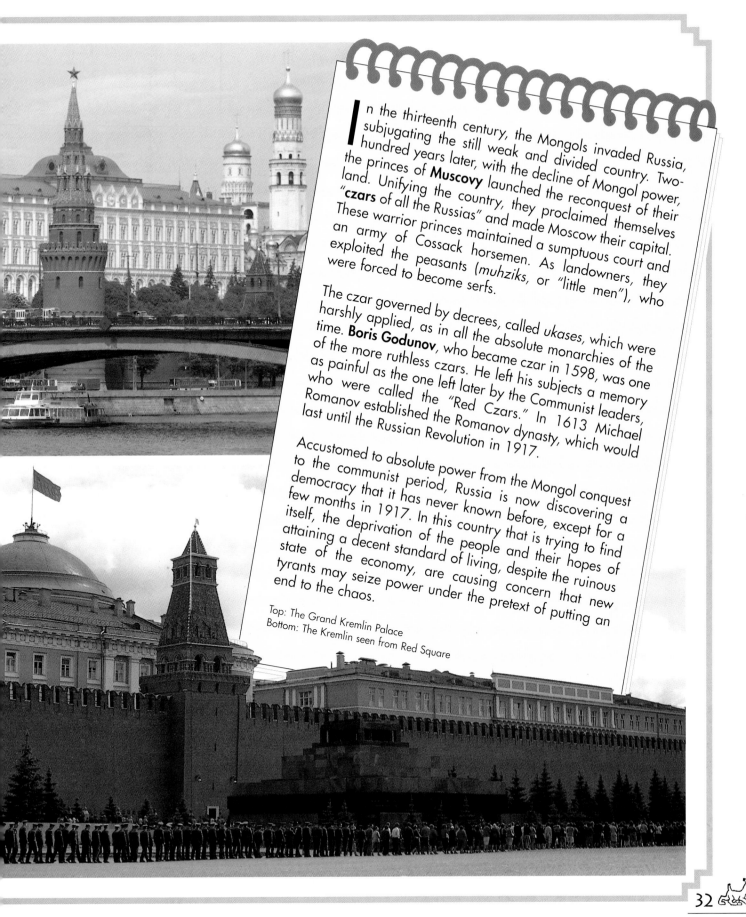

In the thirteenth century, the Mongols invaded Russia, subjugating the still weak and divided country. Two-hundred years later, with the decline of Mongol power, the princes of **Muscovy** launched the reconquest of their land. Unifying the country, they proclaimed themselves "**czars** of all the Russias" and made Moscow their capital. These warrior princes maintained a sumptuous court and an army of Cossack horsemen. As landowners, they exploited the peasants (muhziks, or "little men"), who were forced to become serfs.

The czar governed by decrees, called ukases, which were harshly applied, as in all the absolute monarchies of the time. **Boris Godunov**, who became czar in 1598, was one of the more ruthless czars. He left his subjects a memory as painful as the one left later by the Communist leaders, who were called the "Red Czars." In 1613 Michael Romanov established the Romanov dynasty, which would last until the Russian Revolution in 1917.

Accustomed to absolute power from the Mongol conquest to the communist period, Russia is now discovering a democracy that it has never known before, except for a few months in 1917. In this country that is trying to find itself, the deprivation of the people and their hopes of attaining a decent standard of living, despite the ruinous state of the economy, are causing concern that new tyrants may seize power under the pretext of putting an end to the chaos.

Top: The Grand Kremlin Palace
Bottom: The Kremlin seen from Red Square

IS RUSSIA A EUROPEAN COUNTRY OR AN ASIAN ONE?

Straddling Europe and Asia, Russia has traditions that are close to those of Western European countries. On the other hand, it is also an Eastern country . . .

R ussia was never part of the Roman Empire, and the Russians have always enjoyed their connection with the East. Invasions by the Huns, the Bulgars, and the Mongols affected culture and traditions, as did relations with the **Byzantine** Empire and the conquest of Siberia and central Asia.

One area of Moscow is still called "the Chinese City" ("Chinatown") and some parts of Russia are home to people of Asiatic origin, such as the Tatars, descendants of the Mongols, who settled in the Crimea or on the banks of the Volga. *

In a country whose main resources were, for a long time, in agriculture or lumber, the rise of the industrial middle class and of free enterprise occurred later than in Western Europe. Although Russia has kept its folklore and its traditions intact and very much alive, it is a fact that many Russians were long ago converted to Western ideas. The subtle blend of Russian originality and European roots is probably one of the charming aspects of the Slavic soul.

*The Asiatic population of the former Soviet Union is growing faster than the European part. By the early part of the next century, it will be the majority population group.

Top: A young Siberian woman in Yakutsk
Bottom: A Samarkand market (Uzbekistan)

WHAT IS LENINGRAD CALLED TODAY?

Since 1991, Leningrad has again been known by the name of St. Petersburg. The city was founded by Peter the Great, a convert to modern ideas who made it his capital.

H oping to encourage Russia to end its opposition to progress and seeking to bring his country closer to mercantile Europe, **Peter the Great** (1672–1725) chose to leave "Asian" Moscow, dominated by the land-owning nobility. He commissioned Western engineers and architects, after going to Europe to learn new techniques and trades himself, and built a veritable "Venice of the North" along the shores of the Baltic Sea, complete with churches and palaces, theaters, and large schools, as well as factories and a modern port.

Despite being open to modern ideas, the czars continued to be authoritarian sovereigns, and wealth remained concentrated in the hands of a minority. During the nineteenth century, the country was shaken by peasant revolts. In the Ukraine, where there was a large Jewish community, persecution and **pogroms** were widespread. In 1905, the first big revolution broke out. It was violently repressed by the army, with the Winter Palace massacre and the mutiny on the battleship *Potemkin*. Czar Nicholas II agreed to set up a parliament, called a *Duma*. Lenin fled to the West, but other **Socialist** leaders, striking workers, and any people suspected of progressivism were shot or deported to Siberia. A sketchy version of a parliamentary system was introduced nevertheless, and from 1906 to 1914 Russia experienced substantial economic development.

Left: The facade of a house in St. Petersburg
Right: The tip of Vasilyevsky Island on the Neva River, St. Petersburg

WHEN DID THE OCTOBER REVOLUTION TAKE PLACE?

Czar Nicholas II abdicated in February 1917. A democratically inclined provisional government was created in March and, in October of the same year, the Communist revolutionaries violently overturned the existing regime.

World War I (1914–1918), in which Russia rallied to the Allied side, greatly added to the poverty and hunger of the people. In Petrograd, after a wave of riots, a government made up of moderate Socialists was put in power. But the influence of the Communists, the **Bolsheviks**, was most common in the soviets, committees composed of soldiers, workers, and peasants. On October 24–25, 1917 by the Julian calendar*, the Communists organized a coup d'état and seized power.

The Bolshevik leaders had to fight the anti-Communists and the armies called "White" to distinguish them from the revolutionary army, nicknamed the Red Army. Under the leadership of Lenin, who wanted to get the economy started again and fight famine, the new leaders organized the farms under collective control and introduced a new economic system and a **bureaucratic** system of government, that was just as authoritarian as that of the czarist regime. Assisted by the secret police and the **commissars** of the people, the Communist Party grew in the factories, the countryside, and the army. Faced with the deterioration of the economy, and to get Russia out of the grips of famine, Lenin was forced to return ownership of the land back to the peasants. After a period of relative liberalization of the economy, Joseph **Stalin**'s rise to power after Lenin's death in 1924 marked the beginning of renewed collectivization of the farms.

*November 6–7 by the Gregorian calendar

Top: October Revolution

Bottom: Statue of Lenin

16

WHAT IS COMMUNISM?

In the nineteenth century, the appalling living conditions of the workers inspired many philosophers who were repulsed by the injustice. A German, Karl Marx, devised a theory aimed at abolishing the exploitation of workers.

In **Karl Marx**' view, expressed in his books *The Communist Manifesto* and *Das Kapital*, society is divided into two classes: that of the "haves," the capitalists with money, and that of the **proletarians**, who have no means of survival other than the sale of their ability to work. According to Marx, this inequitable system, which he called **capitalism**, can only add to the privileges of the rich while leaving the poor stagnating in poverty. So that each person can live by working and be neither exploited nor exploiting, social differences must be abolished. Businesses, equipment, and farmland must belong to everyone. Power must be in the hands of those who produce wealth through their labor. Representatives of the proletariat have the responsibility of distributing to each person what he or she needs, and services such as health and education are free.

Coming to power in 1917, Lenin and his followers tried to make the theory a reality. Believing that the population lacked the "maturity" to understand what it needed, the Communist Party became an authoritarian guide, giving rise to the repression of every opposition movement by censure and police surveillance from the redoubtable **Cheka**. Imprisonment and extermination of political opponents in the name of the "dictatorship of the proletariat" caused the regime to degenerate into a police state. From Joseph Stalin to Mikhail Gorbachev in 1985, who was the first leader to lift the restraints, millions of deaths and a ruinous economy were the price paid for insisting, come what may, on trying to turn a utopia into reality.

"Workers of the world, unite!" This statement ends the Communist Manifesto, written by Karl Marx and Friedrich Engels, published in 1848.

40

41

17

WHAT IS PERESTROIKA?

Perestroika (reconstruction of the economy) and glasnost (a policy of freedom of expression) are the two great reforms proposed in 1985 by Gorbachev. But they could not prevent the split of the U.S.S.R.

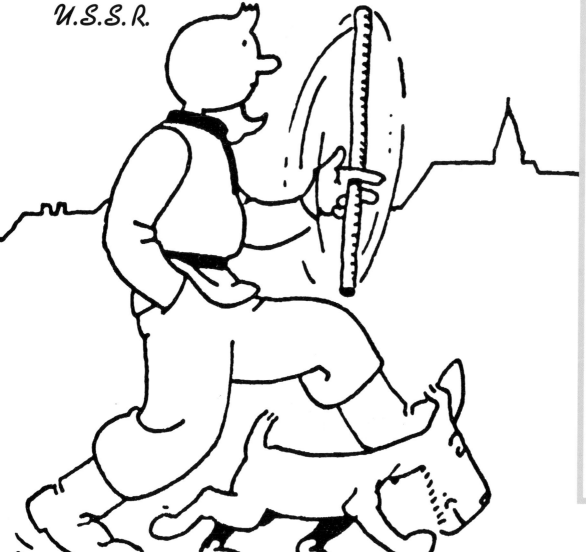

From the 1970s, the U.S.S.R., whose economy had completely deteriorated, could no longer afford the enormous cost of the arms race and the "Cold War." It therefore began negotiations with the United States for the reduction of their respective nuclear arsenals, thus beginning détente, the easing of tensions between the East and West.

With the Helsinki agreements in 1975, the West agreed to resume economic cooperation in exchange for respect for human rights in the U.S.S.R. The Soviet people, however, angered by the inability of the state to improve their standard of living, hungry for freedom, and infuriated by the privileges enjoyed by those favored by the regime, were impatiently calling for radical change.

The reforms launched by Mikhail Gorbachev came too late and were too limited to succeed. In 1991, Boris Yeltsin, elected president of Russia and supported by the population, buried communism. The Soviet Union split into 15 independent republics to be known as the Commonwealth of Independent States (C.I.S.). What will Russia be like tomorrow? No one can say. Russians are discovering freedom, but will they be able to pay the price of improving their economy and still manage to remain democratic?

Top: A handshake between Presidents Reagan and Gorbachev
Bottom: Cheese seller in an outdoor market in Moscow

18

WHERE IS TAMERLANE'S TOMB?

In Uzbekistan, the huge mausoleum of Timur the Lame, known as Tamerlane, is the pride of Samarkand. A ruthless conqueror, Tamerlane remains for the inhabitants of Russian Turkestan the symbol of their past glory.

In central Asia, Turkmenistan, formerly a Soviet country that was also known as Russian Turkestan, is an arid land with no fewer than three deserts: the Kara Kum (black desert), the Kyzyl Kum (red desert) and the Betpak-Dala. Several regions, however, get their water from rivers that rise in the high mountains of Pamir, or have been artificially irrigated since ancient times. These regions have experienced extraordinary civilizations.

Conquered first by the Mongols (Ghengis Khan), then ruled by **Tamerlane** (1369), the five groups of people of Russian Turkestan (Kazakhs, Uzbeks, Tajiks, Turkmen, and Kirghiz) have retained their Islamic religion. Though annexed by the czars of Russia, then attached to the U.S.S.R., they have not forgotten their prestigious past. Their five republics, now independent, have succeeded in safeguarding, in addition to their pride, the busy atmos-phere of the picturesque **souks** and regular attendance at the ceramic-decorated mosques. These countries are famed for their sheep's wool, their valuable carpets, and their orchards. They are also modern countries in which a large network of railroads serves major industrial centers and large cotton plantations. The only shadow cast over the picture is the existence of local criminal organizations, often set up by former Communist leaders, which threaten the economic development of these new countries.

Top: The medersa Chir-Dor in Samarkand

Bottom: Children on the Silk Road

19

WHO LIVES IN THE CAUCASUS?

Small tribes, pushed back by their more powerful neighbors and desperately clinging to their last refuge, have poured into the valleys of the Caucasus, the highest mountain chain in Europe.

Located where Europe and the Middle East meet, the mountains of the Caucasus are home to people from many different areas. In the south, the Georgians settled in ancient times. They are Christian and live in a country with a Mediterranean climate that is famous for its wine, its fruit, and its centenarians.

The Armenians, who are also Christian, were conquered many times in their history, most recently by the Turks during World War I. Peasants, craftsmen, and skillful merchants, they are proud of their ancient culture.

The Azeris of Azerbaijan are Muslim Turks who are strongly influenced by their neighbors in Iran. Their desert country allows for little more than sheep farming, but the Baku oil wells, located on the Caspian Sea, are the oldest in the world and are still being worked.

The Caucasus also shelters people from the farthest limits of Asia, like the Ossets and the Kalmuks. These communities, sometimes consisting of only a few thousand members each, have their own languages and their own traditions. Jealously guarding their independence, and cramped in their tiny territories, they sometimes have trouble avoiding ethnic problems.

Left: Caucasus Mountains in Georgia
Right: A market in Georgia

20

WHICH RAILROAD IS THE LONGEST IN THE WORLD?

Built nearly a century ago, the Trans-Siberian is the longest railroad in the world. It is 6,250 miles (10,000 km) from Moscow to Vladivostok, and the journey takes a week . . . . .

On March 17, 1891, Czar Alexander III ordered the construction of the longest railroad in the world—6,250 miles (10,000 km) of exploration and surveys through forests and mountains and over rivers and endless steppes. The extraordinary construction project took 20 years and was completed in sections. It is said that the human cost was one man's life for every mile. Prisoners and exiles, peasants and soldiers, Chinese laborers and Mongolian nomads all took part, willingly or not, in the gigantic construction effort.

To cross Siberia, solutions had to be found to the serious problems of shortages of water and food supplies, and to the lack of adequate materials, such as high quality wood, which had to be brought in by convoys. Cholera, plague, and temperature extremes—104°F (40°C) in summer and –76°F (–60°C) in winter—also had to be faced.

In this huge territory, 20 times the size of Texas, still half-wild and afflicted with an unrelenting climate, lie hidden fabulous mineral and energy resources that Russia has hardly begun to extract: coal, oil, iron, gold…. Siberia may some day be one of the richest areas of the globe.

Top and bottom left: Russian trains
Bottom right: The church car on the Trans-Siberian railroad, nineteenth century

21

WHO ARE THE GREAT RUSSIAN NOVELISTS?

With novelists like Gogol, Tolstoy and Dostoyevsky, Russian literature in the nineteenth century was one of the richest in the world.

Russians still read the works of their great writers with as much passion as ever, but Communist Russia exerted ruthless censure against writers who criticized the regime. Great novelists like Boris Pasternak and Alexander Solzhenitsyn, the poet Osip Mandelshtam, and the scientist Andrei Sakharov, unanimously respected in the West, were considered reactionaries in the eyes of the party censors. Their books were officially banned and they were sent to prison, to gulags, or into exile.

Many writers were forced to have their books published secretly. They were the *samisdat*, which means "self-publishing." Others saw their works burned by the secret police, or they stopped writing for fear of persecution. Still others died unknown to anyone, or became insane in psychiatric institutions. The regime had no hesitation in disowning artists who were loyal Communists, at the slightest sign of disagreement with the official party "line." These included the painter and poet Vladimir Mayakovsky and the brilliant filmmaker Sergei Eisenstein.

The years of intolerance were all the more terrible because Russian literature was among the world's richest. Novelists like Maxim Gorky, poets like Alexander Pushkin, and playwrights like Anton Chekhov are among the greatest writers of the nineteenth century.

A grandmother reading to her grandchildren

22

WHAT IS THE BOLSHOI?

The Bolshoi is the most famous of the great ballet companies. Acclaimed abroad as well as in Russia, its repertoire consists of works by the five great Russian composers of the nineteenth century.

Cherished as national heroes, Glinka, Borodin, Rimsky-Korsakov, Mussorgsky, and Tchaikovsky revealed to Europe the extraordinary musical heritage of traditional Russia. The whole of the Russian soul is expressed through their works, inspired by Eastern Orthodox church hymns, folk songs from the Russian countryside, gypsy dances, the folklore of Asian people, the choirs of the Volga boatmen, and nostalgic ballads with balalaika accompaniment.

Russians adore shows, and their composers have created many operas and ballets. Diaghilev's *Ballets Russes*, with his interpretations of the modern works of Stravinski, enjoyed great success in Europe in the years before World War I. Since then, Russia has continued to produce composers of great talent, like Prokofiev, as well as virtuoso musicians and fabulous dancers like Rudolf Nuryev and Mikhail Baryshnikov. It also has many troupes specializing in the folklore of its various peoples, to say nothing of the amazing artists of the world-famous Moscow Circus.

Left: A ballerina from the Bolshoi   Right: Young ballet students

23

WHAT ARE THE RUSSIANS' FAVORITE PASTIMES?

Because the Russian summer is so short, not a single minute of it can be wasted. Swimming, fishing, picnics, and long hikes are pleasures that are greatly appreciated before the long winter returns.

The beaches of the Crimea and the Baltic, the pleasure boats sailing the waters of the great rivers, the mountain landscapes of the Urals and the Caucasus, and the vast forests attract crowds of Russians who love the outdoors, the wilderness, and family outings.

The Communist regime was always very careful to offer this sports-loving people a broad range of activities: national football, gymnastics, wrestling, and other athletic activities. Sports competition was carefully organized and led to a very high level of performance. The people were thrilled to amass great numbers of medals at international meets like the Olympic Games. In Russia, skiing, luge, and ice skating hold the place of honor for five to seven months of the year, and at 68°F (20°C) below zero, the "walrus club" proudly breaks the river ice to go swimming. During long winter evenings, chess, another national sport, and reading the great Russian authors are still enjoyed. Shows with traditional folk music and dances, the ballet, plays, and the circus, a big favorite of the Russians, have regained authenticity of expression since the end of the Communist regime.

Left: Playing chess in St. Petersburg
Right: A beach on the Neva River in St. Petersburg

24

WHAT IS AN ISBA?

For centuries, peasants have built their isbas with wood. These solid log cabins, typical of the Russian countryside, are often carefully decorated and painted in bright colors.

For many years wood was the only construction material available to Russian architects, whether they were building a **dacha**, the ramparts of the Kremlin, a palace, or an Eastern Orthodox church with its splendid onion domes. The Russian dwelling gained little from the gradual adoption of brick, stone, and eventually, reinforced concrete. The communist era is characterized by the heavy, imposing style of its official monuments and buildings.

Today, finding a place to live is an ongoing problem, for the cities have grown too quickly around the industrial centers. Though the state invested enormous sums in dams, industrial complexes, and other civilian or military projects, private housing did not keep up. Several families are often crammed together in tiny, poorly-equipped apartments in concrete buildings.

Still, many Russians have been able to acquire a small piece of land on which they build a dacha and cultivate their vegetable gardens on weekends.

Top and bottom left: Typical country houses
Bottom right: A wooden church in Karelia

25

WHAT DO PEOPLE EAT IN RUSSIA?

The food stores are famous for their empty shelves, their endless waiting lines, and the poor quality of their products.

Traditional Russian cuisine favors plain nourishing dishes over sophisticated recipes that are based on products that are scarce, if available at all. Soups like borshch (borscht), made with beets, shchi (with cabbage), and selianka (with meat or fish) are often the basis of the meal. They are served with kascha (boiled buckwheat or millet), or a slice of delicious black rye bread, all washed down with kvass, a type of light beer made from fermented barley or rye. Oddly enough, this country where the dishes usually eaten are very plain is famous abroad for a few luxury specialties: zakouski (cocktail delicacies; hors d'oeuvre), blinis (thin, rolled pancakes), and the famous caviar, the treasure from the Caspian Sea.

Finally, how could we leave out vodka, a grain or potato alcohol that the Russians consume in such quantities that alcoholism has become a major social problem. Since 1992, however, a bottle of vodka has cost the equivalent of a quarter of the average monthly salary, so its consumption has fallen sharply.

Top: Vegetable seller in Moscow
Bottom: Lining up to buy American ice cream in Moscow

26

IS RUSSIA A POOR COUNTRY OR A RICH ONE?

Although Russia is a country rich in natural resources, a citizen's standard of living is often the same as that in a poor country, largely as a result of disastrous management by the former Communist leaders.

B efore the discovery and development of the enormous resources in the Siberian subsoil, the U.S.S.R. already had powerful industrial areas that were rich in iron, coal, and oil. Absolute power, however, exercised by often incompetent politicians who mismanaged the economy, led to the squandering of a good part of this wealth.

Although inspired by a concern for equality, abolition of private profit only discouraged Soviet citizens who wondered, what is the use of effort unless it changes the standard of living? Even the very official cult of "worker heroes," of which the famous **Stakhanov** remains the symbol, was not enough to make up for the ever more pronounced depression of the citizens, embittered by poor working conditions and lack of freedom, and scandalized by the privileges enjoyed by the nomenklatura, the regime's officials.

The only activities that thrived were corruption, the black market, and other forms of trafficking that enable the least scrupulous to improve their lot at the expense of the community.

Left: The Monastery of the Trinity of St. Serge in Sergiyev Posad (Zagorsk)
Right: Precious stones

27

WHO WAS THE FIRST MAN IN SPACE?

In 1961 the Russians sent a man into space for the first time—Yuri Gagarin circled the earth in one hour and thirty minutes.

A stunning proof of the Red Army's technological lead, the October 1957 launch of Sputnik, the first manmade satellite, fired everyone's imagination—the era of space conquest had begun!

Some sectors of the Soviet economy were indeed productive. Taking priority over everything, the army amounted to a "state within the state." There were no shortages for military factories, shops, and personnel. By taking the lead in space conquest, the Soviet regime was reminding the world that Russia was one of the two top world powers.

The first cosmonaut, Yuri Gagarin, in 1961, the first space walk in 1965, the first in-orbit meeting in 1967, the assembling of space laboratories, and the Soviet rockets launched from the Baikonur base (Cosmodrome) in the Kazakhstan desert, have significantly contributed to man's space adventure. By launching hundreds of spy satellites, however, and providing themselves, like the United States, with thousands of nuclear missiles, the U.S.S.R. also helped to endanger the planet. Today, détente, followed by the shattering of the Union and the disintegration of the Communist Party have considerably slowed down the arms race.

Left: Yuri Gagarin
Right: Sputnik III

SPOUTNIK III
15 Mai 1958

28

IS RUSSIA ACCESSIBLE BY SEA?

Russia has many ports, but during the long winter months the ice pack and icebergs prevent access to most of them, thus cutting off the maritime approaches.

Russia has always lived with the fear of naval blockades. Indeed, in winter, ice cuts off access to the ports of St. Petersburg on the Baltic, Vladivostok on the Sea of Japan, and ports on the Arctic Ocean.

Thus, since the time of the czars and later, under the communist regime, the Russians have tried to ensure that their naval bases would be accessible all year long, either by means of alliances, like the one with Cuba, or by annexing the port of Kaliningrad, which was German until World War II.

Despite difficulties with its ports, Russia has one of the largest fleets in the world. Besides warships and merchant vessels sailing every sea on the globe, there are the ships—sometimes very large—that fish or move passengers or goods on the inland seas (the Caspian Sea, Lake Baikal, etc.) or on the great rivers of Russia and Siberia.

The port of Listvyanka of Lake Baikal

29

WHAT HAPPENED AT CHERNOBYL?

In 1986, the fire at this decaying nuclear power station caused a meltdown and seriously irradiated a whole region in the Ukraine and in Byelorussia. Today, protection of the environment is still only a secondary concern in Russia.

The terrible catastrophe at Chernobyl, of which the most seriously affected victims are still dying from radiation-induced cancers, is the horrible result of the leaders' lack of foresight in not building sufficient concrete casing around the reactor. The population was warned of the danger too late, and the true consequences of the accident will not be known until a few more years have passed.

In the eyes of the Soviet officials, industrial progress was more important than the natural setting or the safety of the population. The effect of this policy is that even now several ill-designed nuclear power stations are still endangering the lives of the people living near them. Moreover, a number of polluting industries have been able to settle near large cities. Finally, agriculture is still abusing chemical fertilizers and the big river development works are interfering with the natural balance of immense regions.

One of the most serious dangers is the draining of the Aral Sea. To irrigate cotton fields in Uzbekistan and Kazakhstan, the authorities diverted the waters of the two great rivers of Central Asia: the Syr-Darya and the Amu-Darya, which used to feed this inland sea, the size of the state of Indiana and now in danger of becoming a desert by the year 2000.

The disaster at Chernobyl

30

WHAT IS "BLACK EARTH"?

"Black earth" is a very fertile soil favorable for growing wheat.
Because of it, the Ukraine has long been the rich "storehouse of the U.S.S.R."

B efore 1917, Russia was one of the world's main exporters of grain but they still did not have enough to supply their people, and it was partly in order to get supplies of wheat from the United States that the U.S.S.R. was forced to initiate a policy of détente.

Soviet agriculture lacked neither manpower nor land; it was freedom that was missing. Stalin deported and eliminated several million productive small landowners. Angered by collectivization of their land, the peasants were hardly enthusiastic about working in the **sovkhozy** and **kolkhozy**. The greater part of their time and experience was devoted to the small vegetable gardens left to them by the state for their personal needs or for the sale of the surplus on the free market. Potatoes and cabbages were the most common vegetables in these gardens while the official farms grew mainly grains and plants for industry, such as cotton, sugar beet, and sunflowers, from which the oil is extracted.

Animal husbandry remains underdeveloped, except for horse raising, which has always been practiced on the steppes of Central Asia, and raising sheep, such as the famous *karakul*, a curly-fleeced sheep that gives astrakhan wool.

Top: The steppes in the Ukraine
Bottom left: Wheat field in the Ukraine
Bottom right: A Russian farmer

A

ATTILA (c. 395–453) **:** king of the Huns. Living in what is now Hungary, he attacked the Eastern Empire, invaded the Balkans, conquered the Germans and the Slavs, invaded Gaul, and headed for Italy. His empire collapsed after his death.

B

BOLSHEVIKS : Extremists who, in 1917, favored overthrowing the government by force through revolution.

BORIS GODUNOV (c. 1555–1605) **:** proclaimed czar, he colonized Siberia and tried to bring Russia and the West closer together. The famine that ravaged his country toward the end of his reign resulted in an insurrection during which his son and successor was killed.

BORSHCH (BORSCHT) : type of cabbage and beetroot soup enriched with sour cream.

BUREAUCRACY : a hierarchy of authority with government, often with an unreasonable adherance to rules.

BYZANTIUM : city chosen as capital of the Roman Empire by Constantine I and renamed Constantinople in his honor. It became the capital of the Byzantine Empire, then capital of the Ottoman Empire under the name *Istanbul*.

C

CAPITALISM : economic system in which production is privately owned and prices are determined by competition in a free market.

CHEKA : Soviet political police, created on Lenin's orders on December 20, 1917, officially authorized to convict and execute without referral to the revolutionary courts.

COLD WAR : after 1945 and for 40 years, the U.S.S.R., a supporter of communism, and the United States, a supporter of capitalism, caused a state of constant confrontation to prevail; this was nicknamed the "Cold War." Without daring to set off a nuclear war that would have destroyed the planet, the two powers maintained gigantic military potential and confronted each other through intervening countries.

COMMISSAR : from 1917 to 1946, the head of a department of the government in the U.S.S.R.

COMMUNISM : in theory, an economic system in which production and services are owned by the community.

CZAR : Slavic word, from the Latin "caesar." Name given to the former emperors of Russia.

D

DACHA : Russian country house.

E

EASTERN ORTHODOX : religion with the same beliefs as Roman Catholicism except for the concept of Hell, the Immaculate Conception, and the supremacy of the pope.

G

GENGHIS KHAN (c. 1167–1227) **:** master of all Mongolia. After uniting all the nomadic tribes, he had himself dubbed "supreme chief." He conquered the neighboring settled countries: China, Afghanistan, and all of Persia.

GRAND ARMY (GRANDE ARMÉE) : starting on June 24, 1812, 400,000 men, out of the 600,000 that Napoleon had assembled in the East, entered Russia. Over 20,000 horses were required to pull 1,000 pieces of artillery and their supplies. The cavalry had almost 70,000 horses. The Army was defeated, leading to Napoleon's eventual downfall.

GULAGS : concentration camps to which political prisoners were exiled. They became the symbol of oppression in the U.S.S.R.

I

ICE PACK : accumulation of floating ice forming a huge ice floe.

ISBA : small house built of pine wood, peculiar to the peasants in northern Russia.

K

KOLKHOZ : collective farm in the U.S.S.R. where the land, the farm buildings, the equipment, and some of the cattle are common property.

L

LENIN (VLADIMIR ILYICH) (1870–1924) : Russian revolutionary politician who constantly studied the theoretical principles of Marxism in order to apply them to politics. He was the theoretician, strategist, and tactician of the first Socialist revolution.

M

MARX (KARL) (1818–1883) : German philosopher, economist, and politician whose theories and writings (*The Communist Manifesto* and *Das Kapital*) led to the birth of communism in the world.

MUSCOVY : name given to the principality of Moscow until the seventeenth century.

N

NAPOLEON I (1769–1821) : born in Corsica to a family of moderately high social status, he was crowned emperor by the pope on December 2, 1804. With the dream of building a great empire, he led his armies to victory in Austria, Prussia, and Poland. His first defeat came in 1812 with the retreat from Russia. After being defeated at Waterloo in June 1815, he was exiled by the British to the island of St. Helena, where he died six years later.

P

PETER THE GREAT (1672–1725) : born in Moscow. Convinced of the need for reform, he visited Holland, England, and Vienna, studying shipbuilding and industry. Firmly believing that Westernization of Russia would be achieved mainly through access to and control of the Baltic, he seized the city of Nieuschantz and founded a port that was later to become his capital, St. Petersburg.

POGROM : organized massacres and looting of Jewish communities in Russia in the late 1800s and early 1900s. About two million Jews fled to the United States to escape this persecution.

PROLETARIANS : industrial workers who sell their labor.

R

RATIONALISM : doctrine according to which all certain knowledge is the result of reason.

RURIK : Varangian prince who died in A.D. 879. He founded the principality of Novgorod, the embryonic state of Russia.

S

SCYTHIANS : people of Iranian origin living on the steppes north of the Black Sea.

SOCIALIST : follower of socialism, the belief that the government should own and produce all goods and services and the people in the society should share the work and the products.

SOUKS : marketplaces.

SOVKHOZ : pilot farm belonging to the state.

STAKHANOV (1905–1977) : Soviet miner. During the night of August 30–31, 1935, he dug out 102 tons of coal in six hours, fourteen times the normal amount. Such exceptional results were encouraged by the so-called "Stakhanovist" movement.

STALIN (JOSEPH DZHUGASHVILI) (1879–1953) : unchallenged head and absolute master of the U.S.S.R. after Lenin's death, he imposed his policy of industrialization and enforced collectivization of agriculture. In 1934 he started a huge party purge. During the Stalin era, one million people were executed by firing squads and nine million "enemies of the party" were detained in prisons and concentration camps, according to generally accepted estimates.

STEPPE : large, uncultivated, treeless plain, with a dry climate and sparse, grassy vegetation.

T

TAIGA : coniferous forest (fir, pine, spruce) on the edge of the tundra. It is the world's largest forest.

TAMERLANE (1336–1405) **:** from *Timur lenk, Timur the Lame*. He put an end to the power of the Mongols, had himself proclaimed Muslim sultan, and began the conquest of central Asia, Iran, Syria, and the European part of Turkey. He seized Delhi and was preparing to attack China, but he died before he could carry out his project.

TUNDRA : Lapp term. Steppe in the Artic zone, where the earth is deeply frozen part of the year. The vegetation consists of groupings of mosses and lichens, heathers, and a few herbaceous plants.

B.C.
2000

Slavs from the East descend toward
the Black Sea.

Aryans settle in India (1300)

1000

Encounter with nomads from Asia:
Scythians and Sarmatians (800)

Founding of Rome (753)

0

Invasion of the Goths (300)

First invasion of the Roman Empire
by the Huns (395)

500

Relations with Bulgars
Influence of Byzantines (700)
Advent of Rurik, Prince of Novgorod (862)

Fall of Rome (476)
Collapse of Mayan civilization (c. 900)

1000

Conquest of Russia by the Mongols
(1237–1240)

Birth of Genghis Khan (1167)
Travels of Marco Polo (1271–1295)

1500

Reign of Czar Ivan the Terrible
(1547–1584)

Name *America* used for the New World
for the first time (1507)
Balboa discovers Pacific Ocean (1513)

1600

Start of Romanov dynasty (1613)

Navigation acts passed to restrict
colonial commerce (1600)
Pilgrims land in America (1620)

1700

Peter the Great founds St. Petersburg
(1703)
Catherine II, Empress of Russia
(1762–1796)

Revolt of the American colonies,
followed by the War of Independence
French Revolution (1789)
George Washington's proclamation of
neutrality (1793)

1800

Defeat of Napoleon (Berezina, 1812)
Czar Alexander III orders construction
of the Trans-Siberian railroad (1891)

American Civil War (1861–1865)
Invention of the bicycle (1880)

1900
A.D.

October Revolution in Russia (1917)
Germany attacks the U.S.S.R. (1941)
U.S.S.R. launches first manmade satellite (1957)
Gorbachev becomes youngest leader
of the Soviet Union (1985)
Dissolution of the Soviet Union (1991)

World War II (1940–1945)
Creation of the EEC (European Economic
Community) (1957)
First man walks on the moon (1969)

North Pole

NORWAY

SWEDEN

Arctic Ocean

Bering Strait

Baltic Sea

POLAND • **Kaliningrad** FINLAND

• **St. Petersburg (Leningrad)**

Novgorod

Chernobyl

Kiev

Moscow

Dnepr

Don

Crimea

Sea of Azov

Black Sea

Volga

Caucasus
Mountains

Ural

Berezina

Ural
Mountains

▲ 6,217 ft.

Taiga

Central Siberian
Plateau

• **Verkohoyansk**

Western Siberian
Plain

Trans-Siberian

Ob

Yenisei

Steppe

Lena

• **Baku**

Caspian Sea

Aral Sea

• **Baikonur**

Lake
Baikal

• **Samarkand**

MONGOLIA

Gobi

• **Vladivostok**

Sea of Japan

• **Beijing**

IRAN

AFGHANISTAN

CHINA

KOREA

0   1000   2000 Km

1. Lithuania
2. Latvia
3. Estonia
4. Byelorussia
5. Ukraine

6. Moldavia
7. Georgia
8. Armenia
9. Azerbaijan
10. Russia

11. Turkmenistan
12. Uzbekistan
13. Kirghizistan
14. Tajikistan
15. Kazakhstan

RUSSIA

Capital: Moscow
Area: 6,592,850 sq. miles (17,075,400 sq. km)—76% of the total area of the former U.S.S.R.
Population: 151,436,000 (1993 estimate)
Unit of Currency: *ruble*, divided into *kopecks*

index

bibliography

RUSSIA, FOR READERS FROM 7 TO 77

Andrews, William George.
The Land and People of the Soviet Union.
New York: HarperCollins, 1991.

Ayer, Eleanor H.
Boris Yeltsin: Many of the People.
New York: Dillon Press, 1992.

Bobrick, Benson.
*East of the Sun: The Epic Conquest and
    Tragic History of Siberia.*
New York: Poseidon Press, 1992.

Butson, Thomas G.
Gorbachev: A Biography.
New York: Stein and Day, 1985.

Brighton, Catherine.
*Nijinsky: Scenes From the Childhood
    of the Great Dancer.*
New York: Doubleday, 1989.

Caulkins, Janet.
Joseph Stalin.
New York: F. Watts, 1990.

Erickson, Carolly.
Great Catherine.
New York: Crown Publishers, 1994.

Fannon, Cecilia.
The Soviet Union.
Vero Beach, FL: Rourke Corp, 1990.

Flint, David.
The Russian Federation.
Brookfield, CT: Millbrook Press, 1992.

Fedosiuk, Iurii.
*Hippocrene Insiders' Guide to Moscow,
    Leningrad, and Kiev.*
New York: Hippocrene Books, 1989.

Joseph, Joan.
Peter the Great.
New York: J. Messner, 1968.

Kallen, Stuart A.
Gorbachev/Yeltsin: The Fall of Communism.
Edina, MN: Abdo & Daughters, 1992.

Major, John S.
The Land and People of Mongolia.
New York: Lippincott, 1990.

Mayhew, James.
Koshka's Tales: Stories from Russia.
New York: Kingfisher Books, 1993.

Rawcliffe, Michael.
Lenin.
London: B. Batsford, 1988.

Roth, Susan L.
Marco Polo.
New York: Doubleday, 1990.

Terras, Victor.
A History of Russian Literature.
New Haven: Yale University Press, 1991.

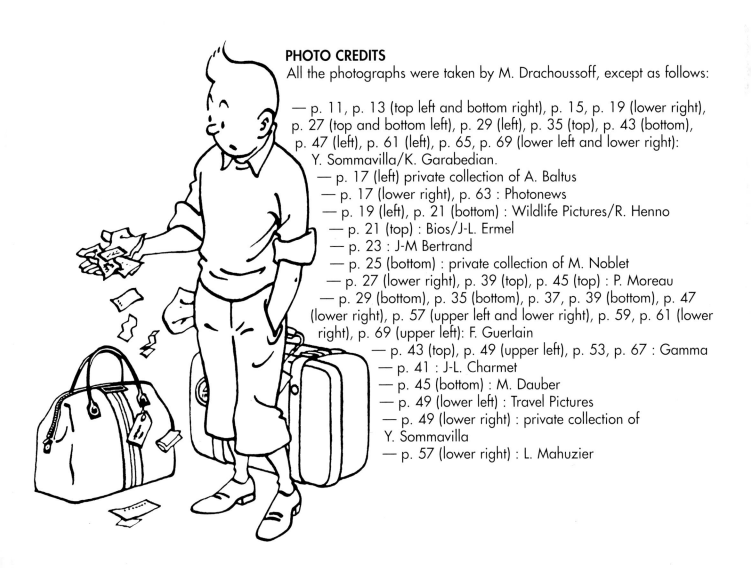

PHOTO CREDITS

All the photographs were taken by M. Drachoussoff, except as follows:

— p. 11, p. 13 (top left and bottom right), p. 15, p. 19 (lower right), p. 27 (top and bottom left), p. 29 (left), p. 35 (top), p. 43 (bottom), p. 47 (left), p. 61 (left), p. 65, p. 69 (lower left and lower right): Y. Sommavilla/K. Garabedian.
— p. 17 (left) private collection of A. Baltus
— p. 17 (lower right), p. 63 : Photonews
— p. 19 (left), p. 21 (bottom) : Wildlife Pictures/R. Henno
— p. 21 (top) : Bios/J-L. Ermel
— p. 23 : J-M Bertrand
— p. 25 (bottom) : private collection of M. Noblet
— p. 27 (lower right), p. 39 (top), p. 45 (top) : P. Moreau
— p. 29 (bottom), p. 35 (bottom), p. 37, p. 39 (bottom), p. 47 (lower right), p. 57 (upper left and lower right), p. 59, p. 61 (lower right), p. 69 (upper left): F. Guerlain
— p. 43 (top), p. 49 (upper left), p. 53, p. 67 : Gamma
— p. 41 : J-L. Charmet
— p. 45 (bottom) : M. Dauber
— p. 49 (lower left) : Travel Pictures
— p. 49 (lower right) : private collection of Y. Sommavilla
— p. 57 (lower right) : L. Mahuzier

Titles in the *Tintin's Travel Diaries* series:

Africa
The Amazon
China
Egypt
India
Peru
Russia
The United States

Wickliffe Elementary School
1821 Lincoln Rd.
Wickliffe, OH 44092